I0107464

CHRIST OR CAESAR

BY

WILLIAM LYON PHELPS

Copyright © 2013 Read Books Ltd.
This book is copyright and may not be
reproduced or copied in any way without
the express permission of the publisher in writing

British Library Cataloguing-in-Publication Data
A catalogue record for this book is available from the
British Library

Contents

William Lyon Phelps

William Lyon Phelps was born on 2nd January 1865, in New Haven, Conneticut, United States.

Phelps earned a B.A. in 1887, writing his thesis on the Idealism of George Berkeley. He then gained an M.A. in 1891 from Yale and his PhD from Harvard in the same year. During his time a Yale, he offered a course in modern novels which brought the university considerable attention both nationally and internationally. This was quite controversial at the time and Phelps was pressured to give up the course, but eventually, due to popular demand, reinstated it outside the official curriculum.

In 1892, Phelps married Annabel Hubbard, sister of childhood friend Frank Hubbard, and the couple moved to the family estate overlooking Lake Huron. Phelps christened it "The House of the Seven Gables", after the Nathanial Hawthorne story of the same name.

He became a very popular figure at Yale but also as an inspirational orator. He went on lecture tours that drew large audiences, speaking on the virtues of modern literature. He also preached regularly at the Huron City Methodist Episcopal Church and attracted such large crowds that the church was remodelled twice in five years to accommodate them.

Phelps published many essays on modern and European literature, including titles such as *Essays on Modern Novelists* (1910), *Some Makers of American Literature* (1923), and *As I Like it* (1923).

After his retirement from Yale in 1933, after 41 years of service, Phelps continued his public speaking, preaching, and writing a newspaper column. He also sat on book selection committees and acted as a judge for the Pulitzer Prize for literature.

His wife, Annabel, died from a stroke in 1939 and Phelps died four years later, in 1943.

CHRIST OR CAESAR
By William Lyon Phelps

"Our country! In her intercourse with foreign nations may she always be in the right; but our country, right or wrong."
"My son! may be succeed in business honestly; but honestly or dishonestly, may be succeed." "My college! may she win all her football games fairly; but fairly or foully, may she win."

I

TODAY the Religion of Nationalism is the most widespread and the most powerful religion in the world. The War of 1914-1918, instead of strengthening the spirit of internationalism and the brotherhood of man, gave an immense impetus to nationalistic fervour. Today Europe is filled with assertive and selfconscious states, and these states are filled with men and boys who will eagerly throw away their lives to obtain or preserve a certain name for their locality. Under any name the citizens would be able to work, play, marry and have children, and go about their daily affairs; but they will gladly kill or die to decide whether their country shall be called a Something or Something-else. If any one doubts whether or not the nationalistic spirit is strong in Asia, all one has to do is to look at India, where men are dying daily for what seems to them a sacred and holy cause.

In time of war, the average father is glad to have his son at the front; proud to sacrifice him for his country. The Gold Star mothers are the Saints of Nationalism. Many modern readers deride the Bible story of Abraham and Isaac; they think it abominable that Abraham consented to sacrifice his son for his religion. If he had revolted and said that his own son was dearer to him than his religious faith, he would seem to many modern readers an admirable character. But the very men who most loudly condemn the ethics of that story are the first to sacrifice their own sons for the religion of Nationalism.

There is not a single country in the world today, big or little, which would not instantly send all its healthy young men into the shambles of battle, if the political party which happened to be in control of the government should decide on a declaration of war. Furthermore, it is probable that the majority of these young men would be glad to go, eager to enlist; no other religion, historical or contemporary, can show such universal devotion, such unreserved willingness to die for its tenets.

In comparison, the Christian religion, widespread as it is, has only a minority of adherents, and only a minority of these would give their lives for the faith. Perhaps the most powerful influence in every country is that of the reigning social class. What is "the thing" to do? There is here no comparison possible between the social standing of Nationalism and of Christianity. Imagine if you can a state of things where as many fathers and mothers would be as proud to have their sons foreign missionaries as they are now proud to have them soldiers. In nineteen centuries there has been an enormous rise in the social respectability of the Christian Church; but it by no means has yet reached the social elevation of a military record in time of war.

The destruction of life has always seemed more glamorous than its preservation. An unselfish scientist, traveling into dark regions infested with disease and danger, traveling there for the sole purpose of saving human life, has little glory in comparison with leaders of armies, who travel there for the purpose of destroying as many human lives as possible.

The physician has never had the appeal or the magnetism of the soldier. Not long ago I heard Doctor Charles-Edward Amory Winslow of Yale University give an eloquent address on the vast number of lives saved by the scientific men who had driven out yellow fever and other pestilential diseases. But in the large audience attentively listening, I do not believe there were three men who could have given the name of a single one of these gallant saviours. In Hartford there is a statue erected in honour of the physician who played an important part in the discovery of anesthetics; he was of course one of humanity's greatest benefactors. Not long ago, I was talking with the famous musician, Ossip Gabrilowitsch. He had been in Hartford the day before, and said he had seen this statue in Bushnell Park, but had forgotten the name. "Oh," said I, "that is a statue in honour of the physician who made an independent discovery of anesthetics." "What's his name?" "Well, now, I can't quite remember whether it is Wells or Welch." Mr. Gabrilowitsch burst out laughing. "Isn't it ridiculous? we don't either of us

7

know the name of this great man, but I am sure we could repeat the name of every prominent general in the Civil War." As it is certain that the majority of those who read this page are as ignorant as we were, I will set down here that the name of this man of genius was Horace Wells. I looked it up in an encyclopaedia.

II

WAR has behind it several thousand years of glory. The Old Testament, the poems of Homer and Virgil, the literature of the whole world, have exalted the renown and splendour of armed men. Fighting is an animal instinct, though only human beings have organized it. It is as fundamental in man as is any other powerful instinct, like hunger, lust of the flesh and the lust of fame. But civilization, reduced to its final expression, means simply the control of human instincts. Civilization is a slow process. We must not expect a speedy cessation of war. It may be many centuries before the world sees the dawn of universal peace.

The evil of war brings out the virtue of courage. Whatever we may think of war, we do well to honour individual heroes. On every Memorial Day, even those of us who like myself regard war as a relic of barbarism, as incompatible both with Christianity and with civilization, do well to celebrate the courage of those who died in battle. We are not glorifying war. We are remembering brave men who sacrificed their lives. We humbly and loyally give them our tribute of praise.

What should be the attitude of a Christian minister in time of war? He is a good citizen and a good churchman. He is a patriot and he is a follower of Jesus Christ. His position is a difficult one. It is quite natural, therefore, and what might have been expected, that during the World War some ministers were pacifists and some were exactly the opposite. Men who are hostile to the Christian religion find any stick good enough with which to beat a Christian minister. Therefore, some ministers were attacked for "disloyalty" and some attacked for patriotism. Curiously enough, it was the enemies of Christianity, not its adherents, who attacked those parsons who did not condemn the war.

Now I think something is to be said for these Christian ministers. Although I do not like to see a church turned into a recruiting station, although I do not like to see Caesar usurping the throne of Christ, it must be remembered that Christian ministers as a class are not loafers. They are workers. They are men with disciplined bodies and disciplined minds. If a large group of men, women and children should decide to migrate beyond the frontier, as happened often in the early days of our country, and attempt to settle down in a wilderness, the hardest workers would be the ministers. They do not stand aside and watch the labour of others. In the World War, when nearly every one (women as well as men) was "doing his bit," it seemed intolerable to many Christian ministers to sit in the seat of the scornful; to condemn the energy of these earnest people; to take a superior ethical standpoint, from which to view all the workers. This willingness to co-operate, especially strong in a time of desperation, analogous to the exciting job of putting out a fire, helps to explain, I think, why so many ministers assisted their country in the hour of peril.

Naturally, there were various mental attitudes among those who "helped to win the war." The old hymn says, *Faith of our fathers! we will love Both friend and foe in all our strife; And preach thee, too, as love knows how, By kindly words and virtuous life.*

There were ministers who displayed no hatred to the official enemy; they gave their own efforts to the Red Cross, they took part in the various "drives" for money; they did their best, not their worst. In order to show the extremes taken by certain Christian ministers, I will cite two cases. There was a Baptist minister in New York who howled execrations at the Germans in a manner worthy of the imprecatory Psalms, and who from the pulpit called pacifists "damned cowards."

And there was a Baptist minister in Vermont, who because he conscientiously could not support war, spoke against it from the pulpit. He was arrested, tried, condemned, and sent to prison for fifteen years.

III

CONSIDER the source and the standards of the Christian religion, both of which are to be found in the New Testament. It was Barabbas and not Jesus who was the bad citizen, the agitator. Jesus never attacked the government. The Gospels and the Epistles show no hatred of Rome. Quite the contrary. "Render therefore unto Caesar the things which are Caesar's; and unto God the things which are God's." St. Peter in the Epistle said, "Fear God. Honour the king." The Christian is to be a good citizen, as in general he certainly ought to be. But toward the end of the first century, how different is the attitude! Then the Christian could not be patriotic, could not be a "good" citizen. In the Book of the Revelation, the government is anathema. Why?

Jesus had not concerned himself with politics. His kingdom was not of this world. But in the book of the Acts of the Apostles we find that Luke is anxious to prove Paul's political orthodoxy, and to insist he was not seditious. Furthermore, the Roman officials are represented as admirable men-honest, impartial, tolerant. Repeatedly they saved the life of the great apostle. It is clear from the Epistles that St. Paul believed in good citizenship, and in obedience to civil law.

In the Apocalypse the Christian had to choose between Nationalism and Christianity. And because he put the Christian religion first, he suffered; but his faith triumphed and survived. The security of the Christian Church today has been bought at a fearful price. So long as a Christian had merely to pay tribute money to Caesar, the Christians did not object. But when, toward the end of the century, the attempt was made to force every one to worship the Emperor as a divine being, the Christians revolted. We surely regard Daniel as a hero because he refused to recant his religion, though ordered to do so by the State. Well, the Christians toward the end of the first century refused to worship Caesar.

In Russia today they refuse to worship Lenin. Do American Christians think Russian Christians should put Nationalistic Atheism, the official religion of the Russian government, ahead of their own faith? In the days of the French Revolution, when Christianity was abolished by law and another religion substituted by the official government, what was the duty of Christians?

When in America the Mexican War was in progress, James Russell Lowell attacked it on the ground that war was incompatible with Christianity.

Ez fer war, I call it murder, There you hev it plain an' flat; I don't want to go no furder Than my Testyment fer that; God hez sed so plump an' fairly, It's ez long ez it is broad, An' you've gut to git up airly Ef you want to take in God. Lowell added in a note,

> *The attentive reader will doubtless have perceived in the foregoing poem an allusion to that pernicious sentiment, "Our country, right or wrong." It is an abuse of language to call a certain portion of land, much more, certain personages, elevated for the time being to high station, our country. I would not sever nor loosen a single one of those ties by which we are united to the spot of our birth, nor diminish by a title the respect due to the Magistrate. . . . We are inhabitants of two worlds, and owe a double, but not a divided, allegiance. In virtue of our clay, this little ball of earth exacts a certain loyalty of us, while, in our capacity as spirits, we are admitted citizens of an invincible and holier fatherland. There is a patriotism of the soul whose claim absolves us from our other and terrene fealty. Our true country is that ideal realm which we represent to ourselves under the names of religion, duty, and the like.*

These words were written not by an enthusiast or by a visionary, but by a man of genius who later served his country in high and responsible stations. They are noble words; but we should remember that when saying them Lowell was supported by local public sentiment in New England, where the war was unpopular. It is probable that when Lowell uncompromisingly called war the same as murder, and incompatible with the teachings of Jesus, he sincerely supposed he would never support a war. Yet when the Civil War broke out, Lowell did not call it murder, but supported it with all his power.

During our Spanish War, "Mr. Dooley" ridiculed the undertaking, and the late Professor William Graham Sumner delivered a public lecture called "The Conquest of the United States by Spain." In the Boer War, G. K. Chesterton, Lloyd George, John Morley, Campbell-Bannerman, and other public men attacked the government of their country. In all these instances, conscience triumphed over Nationalism.

IV

ONE of our leading theologians, Professor Douglas Clyde Macintosh, a Canadian by birth, wishes to become a citizen of the United States, but wishes also to reserve the right whether or not to support this country in the event of war, saying he must follow his conscience rather than his possible obligations as a citizen. The judges in the Connecticut Court refused him citizenship, interpreting the law to mean that a foreign candidate must support his adopted country without any reservations. This seemed unfortunate, not for Professor Macintosh, but for the United States; men of high education, of noble character, of sensitive conscience, are best fitted for citizenship, most needed by every country. Yet the law is the law, and it seemed that the Professor had no case at all.

But he appealed; and the higher court in New York, with a unanimous decision of the three judges, admitted the candidate, stating that the Constitution of the United States never intended to interfere with the inalienable rights of conscience. judge Manton said, "They are given by God, and cannot be encroached upon by human authority without. criminal disobedience to the precepts of natural as well as revealed religion." This is a very important decision.

Some years ago when Madame Schwimmer carried a somewhat similar case to the United States Supreme Court, she was denied citizenship, but a dissenting opinion was written by Oliver Wendell Holmes, who said, *Some of her answers might excite popular prejudice, but if there is any principle of the Constitution that more imperatively calls for attachment than any other it is the principle of free thought -not free thought for those who agree with us but freedom for the thought that we hate. I think that we should adhere to that principle with regard to admission into, as well as to life within this country. And recurring to the opinion that bars this applicant's way, I would suggest that the Quakers have done their share to make the country what it is, that many citizens agree with the applicant's belief and that I had not supposed hitherto that we regretted our inability to expel them because they believe more than some of us do in the teachings of the Sermon on the Mount.*

The supreme value of these tests-and perhaps that is why Professor Macintosh insisted, at considerable mental anguish, on appealing his case-is that here the teachings of Christ come squarely and uncompromisingly into conflict with the Religion of Nationalism. When he was forced to choose, the Professor decided he would rather be a Christian than a citizen. He is a Christian first and an American second. Is not that the right order for every true Catholic and every true Protestant?

I believe that in the future the Catholic Church, the best organized form of the Christian religion, will do much toward the abolishment of war. During the World War, George Bernard Shaw declared that if he were the Pope, he would without hesitation immediately excommunicate every Catholic soldier in every country who did not lay down his arms. Well, it is as difficult to imagine what Mr. Shaw would do if he were Pope, as it is to imagine him holding that august office. But his remark emphasized the international nature of the Organized Church.

It certainly seems tragic that in the late war English Catholics gladly butchered Austrian Catholics; and that German Catholics gladly butchered American Catholics. I wonder if the powerful and well-organized Catholic Church Universal will always endure such a state of things?

The fact that such a state of things seemed both inevitable and natural is a proof of the tremendous strength of the Religion of Nationalism. It triumphs over every other bond that unites men. Science, the love of truth, all political organizations, were as powerless against it as was the Church. Socialists in all countries were butchering Socialists in other countries. French research scholars in science were gladly engaged in butchering research scholars of the "enemy." The love of truth was eclipsed by sentimental Nationalism. There were certainly more Christian ministers, however, who sacrificed themselves for the truth than there were scientists. Most of the scientists were engaged in devising more powerful engines of destruction. I can think of only one man of science who put what he regarded as the truth above the emotion of nationalism-Bertrand Russell.

V

PATRIOTISM is a noble and beautiful sentiment, as noble and beautiful as loyalty to one's family. In ordinary circumstances, that is to say in times of peace, can there be any doubt that Christians as a rule are the best citizens? They are the best citizens as they are the best sons, husbands, and fathers. Both country and family receive the devotion of religious men and women. The members of the Church of Christ are law-abiding; they are not criminals. They do their public duty, they individually contribute to the support of the nation, they are for the most part, honest, intelligent, up right, the salt of the earth.

Now although they love their families and their homes, would they cheat, lie, steal or murder in order to help or preserve their families? and would they be praised if they did? They would not. Their religion comes first, their families second.

In America the Fourth of July and the Twenty-fifth of December are both legal holidays. There has been within the last fifty years an elevation in the average mental attitude toward both these days of jubilation. The standard of patriotism and the standard of religion have both risen. Although our age is the age of noise, on one day of the year-the Fourth of July-there is less noise than formerly. We show our patriotism today in a diminishment of gunpowder and in a diminishment of oratory. When I was a boy, there was in every town and village in America a "Fourth of July oration," which the patient populace felt compelled to hear. The muzzle velocity of the orator of the day was tremendous; he roared at the top of his lungs, celebrating with voice and gesture the past, the present, the future of the "greatest nation on the face of the earth." This speaker was chosen not because he had anything to say, but because he excelled his rivals in the ability to maintain a fortissimo.

Well, we have changed all that. Such an oration today would be received either with derisive laughter or with a steadily decreasing number of listeners. This does not mean that we are less patriotic than previous generations; it means that our love of country is not to be measured by rhetorical violence. Furthermore, so many boys (and innocent bystanders) were maimed, blinded, and killed by the indiscriminate use of gunpowder (exclusively for patriotic purposes) that city governments finally came to the conclusion that the display of patriotism must take a more sensible form. Let us hope that the catch-word, a "safe and sane Fourth" may eventually mean a safe and sane mental attitude in all loyalties.

True patriotism, sincere love of one's country ought always and everywhere to be shown not by boastful jingoism, but by manners and conduct that display good breeding.

21

One of the definitions of patriotism in Webster's Dictionary is devotion to the welfare of one's country.

I should like to see all Americans, instead of being proud of having the greatest wealth in the world, or the most powerful navy in the world, or the best climate in the world- I should like to see them proud of belonging to the most unselfish country in the world, the most generous country in the world. I think it is true that Americans are the most amiable of all people, the most good-natured, the most jolly; but I should like to see the word American stand not merely for good-nature, but for good behaviour, for modesty, for kindness, for tolerance, for breadth of mind and culture. We should compete with other countries not in armaments or in riches, but in the fruits of the Spirit.

A man who is truly ambitious does not wish to excel his neighbours in physical strength or in truculence; he does not hope that his neighbours will be afraid of him; he wants them to like him, to admire him, to respect him, to love him, to come to him as to an intimate friend. The same thing applies to one's country. A loyal and patriotic American does not have to wave the flag or beat the drum. He does not wish to have other countries afraid of the United States, to look upon us with distrust, suspicion, and hatred. He wants his country so to behave in the eyes of the world that we shall be the most loved and admired of all nations; that our actions will be better than our words; that we shall always be expected to do the right thing because we are Americans. Whatever sacrifices are involved in gaining the love and respect and confidence of other countries are certainly judiciously made. We cannot afford to insist on the legal pound of flesh at the price of hatred.

VI

Now as there has been an improvement in the significance of the word patriotism and it is certain that in the future the word will reach a still higher elevation, so the connotation of the word religion has of late years been enriched and ennobled. Religion has come to be not primarily an affair of the voice, but of the life. The Master invariably stressed character. Speaking exclusively to his professed disciples, he said, "Why call ye me Lord, Lord, and do not the things which I say?" "Not every one that saith unto me Lord, Lord, shall enter the Kingdom of Heaven; but he that doeth the will of my Father who is in Heaven." Men and women are judged by their lives. The only convincing answer to atheism and scepticizm is to live like a Christian. This is more difficult than to argue with, or to denounce, or to ridicule the atheist; but it is also more effective.

In the same way, the professions of a nation are judged simply and wholly by its conduct. If the official voice of a country proclaims the love of peace and good will and charity and affection for all the nations of the earth, and at the same moment the same country is building up a navy with the intention of having the biggest and most powerful armament in the world, this official voice will be regarded as the voice of a liar. It would really be better not to make any pretty speeches; it would, indeed, be better to speak the truth.

In most nations today the word anarchist has a bad odour; but from the point of view of international law, at this moment every nation in the world is an anarchist. An anarchist is one who believes in absolute individual freedom; who recognizes no law except his own desire. Well, not long ago when it was reported that Japan had made some statement that might be taken as derogatory to the United States, our Senate went on record as declaring that the United States of America could not tolerate any interference or suggestions from any other nation. It is probable that in this very year of grace nothing would be more hotly resented by the majority of our accredited political representatives than a remonstrance or even advice from any other country. What is that but international anarchy?

When a new region is first invaded by settlers, every man is a law unto himself; and every man goes armed. After a time, such a condition of things becomes intolerable; individual license forbids community liberty. Vigilance committees are formed; and in process of time, a central government is established.

All those who insist with such vigour that the United States must on no account enter into any alliance with other nations are really insisting that every nation should be and remain an anarchist. Fortunately, they are also resisting the

Time-Spirit. They are imbedded in the superstitions of the past and are blind to the future. They are looking in the wrong direction. For it is as certain as anything can be that our American descendants will live in a World League.

VII

PROFESSOR ROBERT MILLIKAN, one of the foremost physicists of the world, says in his book Science and the New Civilization that there are three leading ideas in the world of thought and science. First, foremost, and of the highest importance, he puts the Golden Rule. He believes this Law to be more important than the law of gravitation or than the principle of evolution. It is the profoundest truth known to man. The greatest teacher in history not only said "Love thy neighbour as thyself," but in response to the question, "Who is my neighbour?" he left no doubt that our neighbours were all the children of men. The fact that a man lives on the other side of a national boundary line does not cancel his neighbourship, or release us from our neighbourly duty.

Live and let live. Prejudice is an ugly thing and Tolerance a fine thing; but there is something more splendid than tolerance. It is Fellowship.

The actual realization that all the world is one family is the ideal for the true patriot. If the words Fatherhood of God and Brotherhood of Man have any meaning whatever, if they are anything except hypocritical cant, then there can be no such thing as a foreign war. Every war is a civil war.

But not only is international friendship desirable, it has become a necessity. War simply won't do. As the murder of another man's body is the suicide of the murderer's soul, so one nation cannot with spiritual safety destroy another.

The first Fourth of July celebration was in a war. The most "glorious Fourth" in the future will be that one which celebrates, in the language of the poet, The Parliament of Man, the Federation of the World.

VIII

WE CANNOT have the Millennium now, but we can do our best to improve present conditions. For every country at this moment to abolish its army and navy would be as absurd as it would be to abolish courts of law or prisons. Tolstoy, who, like most Russians, was an extremist, insisted on the abolishment of law courts and policemen. But what sensible Christian, remembering the Boston police strike, would advocate that? We are not living, not yet, in Paradise; we must do the best we can in this imperfect world.

Even the most thorough-going idealist must recognize facts- the actual, existing conditions. Aylmer Maude, in the new Centenary Edition of the Works of Tolstoy, writes, Tolstoy stated the case against patriotism and war powerfully, and it was important to have this well done in order to have some literary counterpoise to the patriotic influence exerted by the classics and the Old Testament-books written when people did not know other nations, but sincerely hated them, and when the foreigner was a natural enemy and men believed that their national God abhorred the "Gentiles," and desired to see the Hivites and the Amorites smitten hip and thigh.

Tolstoy showed convincingly that Christianity, with its doctrine of the Fatherhood of God, is fatal to patriotism, and that even those who object to the word "God" and prefer some other phraseology, can frame no rational outlook on life which justifies the sacrifices the modern world offers up on the altar of international jealousy and enmity sacrifices often as reckless and as blind as those that of old were offered to Moloch or to Mars.

What he did not see, however, was the rational basis that exists for national feeling of a non-malevolent kind. If the world is to be organized, law to prevail, and Governments to rest on the will of the people (all things of which we generally approve), then it is practically necessary that the world should be subdivided into kingdoms of manageable proportion, and once such subdivisions exist, it is natural to remember that "charity begins at home," and our first duty is to see that we get things rightly arranged in our own section....

However horrible war may be-and I regard it as on a par with slavery, duelling, and cannibalism-to stop it by the method Tolstoy commends (that of each conscientious man refusing to serve as a soldier or to pay taxes) has the grave disadvantage that if successful it would disintegrate the State, and if attempted by all humane people, would throw the control of affairs into the hands of those who were not humane.

Life is full of perplexities. The relation of a loyal Christian to his country in the next war is not easy to predict;

because no one can read the future. No one knows when the next war will come, or what kind of war it will be. Therefore I myself, as a Christian and a patriot, will refuse to say now that in the future I would never under any circumstances support a war; for I do not know but that I might be forced to choose between two evils. In the Civil War many Quakers fought against slavery. If in this world we could choose only between black and white, how easy our choice would be! But it was Hegel, I believe, who said that in most cases we are forced to choose between Light Brown and Dark Brown; and if we believe, of two courses, that one is fifty-one per cent right, then perhaps that course deserves one hundred per cent of our support. But in all cases I would put the religion of Christ first and everything else second.

IX

IT is often said that people in the Twentieth Century have lost the sense of sin. But Christians who know that their lives are spent in a daily fight against sin, rejoice that in one respect the world has reached a consciousness of sin hitherto not only unfelt, but for the majority of people, unknown.

There is everywhere a growing sentiment that war is sinful. In the Middle Ages, the Christian organizations rejoiced in the slaughter of heathen, the butchery of infidels; they believed their chances for eternal salvation increased in direct proportion to the number of unbelievers they had personally extinguished. In the American Revolution, although some Americans were patriotic rebels and some were patriotic Tories, apparently none believed there was in war itself anything wicked or inconsistent with fervent piety. The same conditions of public opinion existed in our Civil War. Northern orthodox ministers rejoiced whenever Southern church-members were killed; they saw no incongruity between preaching the gospel of Jesus and endeavouring to carry on the war against their brethren in the South. They did everything possible to increase the strength of the fighting spirit in the North. Northern Episcopal clergymen were delighted when that Southern pillar of the church, Bishop Leonidas Polk, was killed in battle.

The standards of the Christian religion have not fallen but risen. During the World War there were not only many Christians who refused to fight under any circumstances, there were thousands engaged in the struggle who constantly felt its incompatibility with the religion they professed, and "carried on" merely to make the best of a bad job. This sentiment has been markedly increased by the books that have multiplied since the war. Any book or any drama today which represented war as sentimentally glorious, would receive almost universal ridicule.

X

MANY enemies of Christianity have declared that the World War destroyed the Christian religion. The Christian prestige was certainly injured by it, as it ought to have been. Many lost their faith. Faith is always dimmed by anything that works against the conception of Triumphant Goodness. But so far from the Christian religion having been destroyed by the late war, I believe it is the other way around. In the long run, it is War and not Christianity which will get the worst of it. Long after war has ceased to be, men will continue to build churches, to read the Gospels, to say their prayers. The personality of Jesus will dominate mankind in the distant future more powerfully than at any period in the past.

Every true Christian is looking fearlessly and confidently forward. We hope not only that America will join other nations in the reduction of armaments, we hope she will lead the way. We should assist every move in the direction of peace; we should take a prominent part in every movement to bring together as in one family all the nations of the earth. The peace-makers are not ridiculous; there is no greater folly than war.

Those who maintain it is hopeless to stop war, that war always has existed and always will exist, are narrow conservatives, devoid of progressive spirit. The same courage and spirit of co-operation that have been employed in the prosecution of war, will some day be employed in attaining and in maintaining peace.

When Thoreau was addressing an audience, he exclaimed, "There's a good time coming, boys!" A certain heckler sneered, "Can you fix the date?" Thoreau replied, "Will you help it along?"

XI

YES, there is a good time coming, "though a battle's to fight ere the guerdon be gained, the reward of it all."

I see unmistakable signs of the coming conflict between the religion of Christ and the religion of Nationalism. The world today is conscious as never before of the sin of war, of its incompatibility with religion, with civilization, with intelligence, with the pursuit of learning, with every true conception of the brotherhood of man.

When this conflict comes- and it is surely coming- then it will cost something to be a Christian, as it did in the first century. The chief difficulty with the Christian Church today is that it means so little. In order that it may rise to its possibilities- for if all Christian church-members united now, war could be prevented- it may be necessary in the future for Christians once more to become unpopular, as they were in the ancient days of persecution, as they were in France in the eighteenth century, as they are now in

Russia. The strength of the religion of Nationalism is shown by the willingness of its followers to sacrifice their lives. If the religion of Christ is to become lusty, it must receive not merely a polite and passive acquiescence, it must demand and receive the supreme sacrifice.

I feel that the Christian Church is once more to be tested. Instead of church membership being a comfortable social asset, it is going to hurt. Then the Christian Church will suffer from persecution and become strong; thousands will leave it as rats leave a sinking ship. They leave it because they are rats. Perhaps it was sinking because it carried too many rats. Perhaps it will sail more buoyantly after the rats have left it.

If there is one thing of which I am certain, it is the ultimate triumph of the principles of the Christian religion. Already it has one great advantage over the religion of Nationalism. The religion of Nationalism is compulsory; those who do not give it first place are forced to do so. But compulsion has never in the long run succeeded.

The religion of Christ is voluntary. Many men and women, many teachers and college professors, any businessman may refuse his allegiance or even defy it with impunity and with security. No citizen is compelled to go to church. The Christian Church is made up wholly of volunteers; there are no drafted men. In this lies its potential strength.

The time is coming when the promise of the First Christmas will be abundantly fulfilled. Then every Christmas will be more than a family celebration, more than a legal national holiday; it will be the realization of peace on earth and good will to men.

THE END

www.ingramcontent.com/pod-product-compliance
Lightning Source LLC
Chambersburg PA
CBHW051741040426
42447CB00008B/1242